KB244197

The Time Machine Bicycle

Happy House

About Wise & Wide

- A systematic 6-level English reading program based on Lexile® measures
- Diverse and interesting topics chosen from the elementary curriculums of Korea and English speaking western countries
- Well-written books in various forms including fiction stories, descriptive texts, and classics retold
- The informative but original fiction stories grab your interest, leading to the easy and clear understanding of the educational content.
- Improve thinking skills with solid after-reading activities at all levels of the series.

Wise & Wide is a 6-level English reading program that consists of 60 books and each level is systematically divided by Lexile® measures. The Lexile® Framework for Reading is the most popular reading measuring system in American formal education curriculums and many English programs. Over 20 out of 50 states in the U.S. mark Lexile® measures directly on students' final report cards and over 300 well-known publishers adopt and use Lexile® measures.

Experience many kinds of readings written by professional writers from the U.S. and England. They used interesting topics that were carefully chosen after analyzing elementary curriculums from around the world including Korea, the U.S., England, and Australia among many others. Comprehensive after-reading activities including graphic organizers, speaking tasks, and After-reading Tests are ready for you.

Levels in the series and their corresponding Lexile® measures

Level	Lexile® measures	U.S. Grade
Level 1	Below 200L	Pre K - K
Level 2	190L - 400L	Lower Grade 1
Level 3	350L - 530L	Upper Grade 1
Level 4	420L - 650L	Grade 2
Level 5	520L - 940L	Grade 3 - 4
Level 6	830L - 1070L	Grade 5 - 6

* Smart Readers: Wise & Wide level 1 is applicable to the preschool level in the U.S.

* The source of the relationship between Lexile® measures and U.S. school grades: CCSS(Common Core State Standards) FOR ENGLISH LANGUAGE ARTS, APPENDIX A (2012, which is used by 45 states in the U.S.)

Topic List

	Level 1	Level 2	Level 3	Level 4	Level 5	Level 6
Book 1	Science>Biology: The hibernation of animals Story	Science>Biology: Living and nonliving things Story	Science>Biology> Animals & the Environment: Sea otters Story	Environment> Living with nature: The diver & the persimmon tree Story	Science>Biology> Animal: Amazing animals of the Amazon Story	Science>Biology: Germs, transmitted diseases Story
Book 2	Literature> World classics: Aesop's fables Story	Literature> Traditional fairy tale: Old tales about stones Story	Social Studies> Economy: To run a business to make and save money Story	Science>Biology> Plants: Photosynthesis Story	Science>Earth science: Earth's layers, earthquakes, volcanoes, and earth's atmosphere Report	Mathematics> Sequence: The golden ratio & the Fibonacci sequence Story
Book 3	Science>Physics: How shadows are formed Story	Literature> World classics: Peter Pan Story	Science>Scientific technology: Nanobots Story	Literature>Myths: World's creation stories Story	Literature> Legend: The story of King Arthur Story	Literature>Myths: Constellation myths Story
Book 4	Literature> Traditional literature: The Talmud Story	Science>Biology> Animal: Polar bears Story	Science>Biology> Animal: Mountain gorillas Story	Social Studies> Cultural anthropology: Amazing ancient cultures of the world Story	Science> Earth science: Clouds and weather Story	Literature> Human & animals: The friendship between a girl and a horse Story
Book 5	Social Studies> Ethics: Rules in daily life Story	Science>Biology: The five senses Report	Social Studies> Cultural anthropology: Astonishing festivals Report	Art>Music: Stories from two operas Story	Social Studies> World culture & history: The Renaissance Story	Sports> Board sports: Surfing & snowboarding Story
Book 6	Social Studies> World geography & travel: Tourist attractions around the world Story	Science>Biology> Animal: Dinosaurs Story	Science> Astronomy: The solar system Story	Social Studies> People: Three great people who overcame hardships Story	Science>Scientific technology: The wonderful world of robots Report	Art>Music: Composers of the Romantic Era Report
Book 7	Science> Space science: The life of astronauts Report	Social Studies> Cultural anthropology: Mythological monsters from around the world Report	Mathematics> Elementary mathematics: Numbers, measurement, shapes and data Report	Science & Social Studies> Technology & culture: Inventions from around the world Report	Art>Works of art: Famous paintings Report	Social Studies> Human & animals: Animals in action for human Report
Book 8	Social Studies> Cultural anthropology: Various living cultures of the world Story	Art>Music: Instruments in the orchestra Story	Social Studies> Life safety: Learning and using outdoor survival skills Story	Social Studies> History: The California Gold Rush Report	Social Studies & Science> Psychology: Psychology in everyday life Story	Literature> World classics: The Merchant of Venice Story
Book 9	Social Studies> Jobs: Interviews about jobs Report	Science>Scientific technology: Developments in technology in different times Story	Social Studies> Politics>Election: Running for 3rd grade class president Story	Literature> World classics: Stories of Sherlock Holmes Story	Literature> World classics: Adrift in the Pacific Story	Social Studies> History & People: Great world leaders in history Report
Book 10	Literature>Traditional fairy tale: Eastern and Western folk tales on the same theme Story	Sports>Winter sports: Various aspects of some Winter Olympic sports Report	Literature> World classics: Short stories by O. Henry Story	Sports> Ball games: Various aspects of popular ball games Report	Social Studies> History: Famous events that changed world history Report	Art & Social Studies> Art: Stories about the creation, distribution, and preservation of paintings Report

* 10 books in each level will be published.

How to Use This Book

•Before Reading

You can easily find the topic and what kind of story you are about to read.

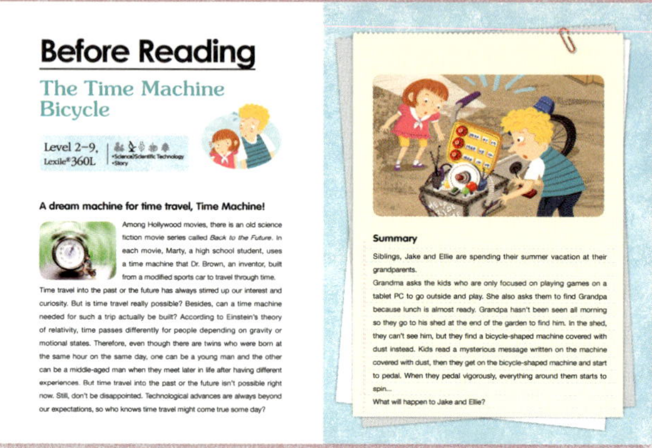

•The text

All the stories were written by professional writers from the U.S. and England, so you will read authentic and appropriate English sentences and expressions in every book in the series.

•Pop Quiz

Check out right away if you understand what you have just read by solving a pop quiz that checks your comprehension.

•Key Words

The key words and expressions on each page are listed for you to easily study them.

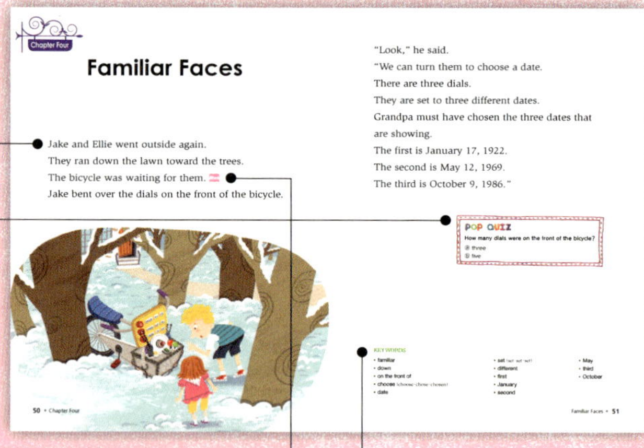

•Aha! Tips

Download free Korean explanations at *www.ihappyhouse.co.kr* for all of the sentences marked with "Aha!". These explain cultural, scientific, and economic knowledge or they deal with aspects of English such as grammatical structures or idiomatic expressions. There are lots of "Aha! Tips" to help you understand the text.

•Comprehension Quiz

After reading one chapter, solve various questions to find out if you fully understand the content.

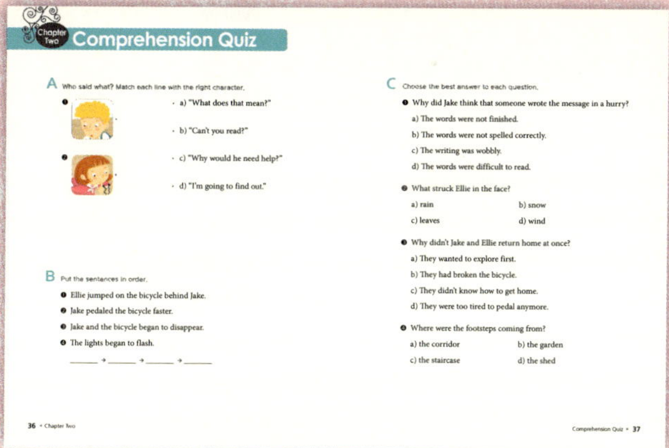

•Let's Review the Story /
•Let's Think & Talk

Fill in the blanks in the organizer to summarize the whole story. Express your own thinking and feelings about the story by answering the questions. You can build up logic and reasoning skills for your essay examinations in the future.

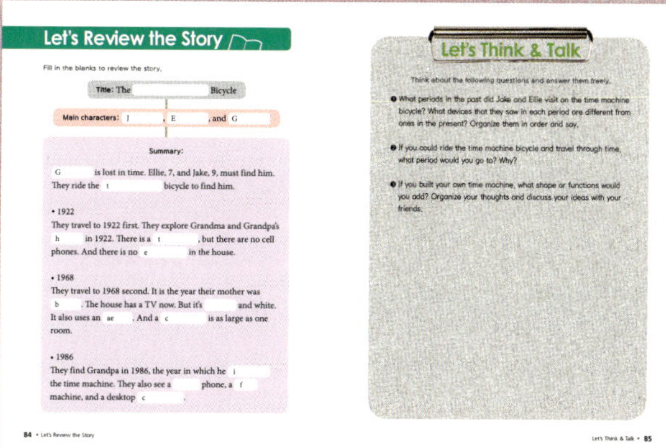

Appendix

Audio CD

In the CD audio book form, the texts are read vividly by American professional voice actors.
(MP3 files downloaded for free)

After-reading Test

Solve an additionally provided After-reading Test for each book.

The Korean translation, Answer Keys, a Word Quiz, a Word List, and Aha! Tips for each book

You can download them for free at *www.ihappyhouse.co.kr* or *www.darakwon.co.kr*

Before Reading

The Time Machine Bicycle

Level 2–9,
Lexile® 360L | •Science〉Scientific Technology
•Story

A dream machine for time travel, Time Machine!

Among Hollywood movies, there is an old science fiction movie series called *Back to the Future*. In each movie, Marty, a high school student, uses a time machine that Dr. Brown, an inventor, built from a modified sports car to travel through time.

Time travel into the past or the future has always stirred up our interest and curiosity. But is time travel really possible? Besides, can a time machine needed for such a trip actually be built? According to Einstein's theory of relativity, time passes differently for people depending on gravity or motional states. Therefore, even though there are twins who were born at the same hour on the same day, one can be a young man and the other can be a middle-aged man when they meet later in life after having different experiences. But time travel into the past or the future isn't possible right now. Still, don't be disappointed. Technological advances are always beyond our expectations, so who knows time travel might come true some day?

Summary

Siblings, Jake and Ellie are spending their summer vacation at their grandparents.

Grandma asks the kids who are only focused on playing games on a tablet PC to go outside and play. She also asks them to find Grandpa because lunch is almost ready. Grandpa hasn't been seen all morning so they go to his shed at the end of the garden to find him. In the shed, they can't see him, but they find a bicycle-shaped machine covered with dust instead. Kids read a mysterious message written on the machine covered with dust, then they get on the bicycle-shaped machine and start to pedal. When they pedal vigorously, everything around them starts to spin...

What will happen to Jake and Ellie?

The Time Machine Bicycle

The Time Machine Bicycle

A Mysterious Message

"Jake, it's my turn to play on the tablet," said Ellie.

"I haven't finished yet," grumbled Jake.

He was nine years old, and had little patience with his seven-year-old sister.

Ellie scowled at her older brother as he bent over his game once more.

"That's not fair.

Grandma said that you could use it for an hour."

She picked up Jake's phone to look at the time.

"You've had it for an hour and a half.

Then, can I use your phone?"

"No, because it needs charging."

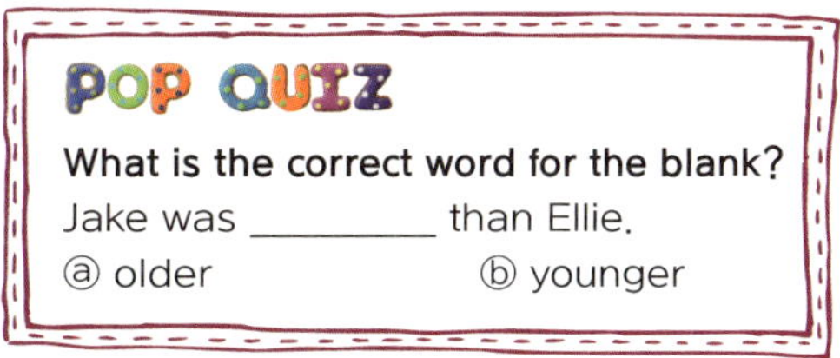

KEY WORDS

- mysterious
- message
- it's my turn to + *Verb*
- play
- on
- tablet
- finish
- yet
- grumble
- *Number* + years old
  (*cf. Number* + -year-old / year)

- have little patience with
  (have-had-had)(*cf.* patience)
- scowl at
- older
- as
- bend over (bend-bent-bent)
  (*cf.* over)
- once more
- fair
- could
- hour

- pick up
- look at
- half
- then
- because
- need
- charging

Jake sighed.

"Why can't we have a tablet each?

Then, we could both play on it all day long.

I can't play Pokémon Go here because the broadband speed is too slow. 

Besides, I've used up my data allowance for this month."

KEY WORDS

- sigh
- each
- both
- all day long
- Pokémon

- here
- broadband
- speed
- too
- slow

- besides
- use up
- data
- allowance
- month

Just at that moment, Grandma came in.

"Why don't you play outside?" she said.

"Go and enjoy the beautiful weather."

The sun poured in through the windows of the
tall, old house.

KEY WORDS

- **just at that moment** (*cf.* moment)
- **come in** (come-came-come)
- **why don't you ~?**
- **outside**
- enjoy
- weather
- pour
- through

Outside, the grassy lawn was bright green.

Birds were singing.

The scent of flowers filled the air.

It was a beautiful English summer.

Mom and Dad were working through the summer vacation.

They could not give up their jobs.

They could not take six weeks off.

So they had sent the children to stay with their grandparents.

"When I was your age…" began Grandma.

Jake cut in rudely.

"Yeah, we know.

When you were our age, you had no computers.

You had no cell phones."

KEY WORDS

- **grassy lawn** (*cf.* grassy / lawn)
- **bright green**
- **sing** (sing-sang-sung)
- **scent**
- **fill**
- **the air**
- **English**
- **work**
- **vacation**
- **give up** (give-gave-given)
- **job**
- **take off** (take-took-taken)
- **week**

- **so**
- **send** (send-sent-sent)
- **stay with**
- **grandparent**
- **when**
- **age**
- **begin** (begin-began-begun)
- **cut in** (cut-cut-cut)
- **rudely**
- **yeah** (= yes)
- **know** (know-knew-known)
- **computer**
- **cell phone**

Grandma sighed.

"Will you two go and see if you can find Grandpa?" she said.

"I haven't seen him all morning. Tell him that lunch will be ready in half an hour."

Grumbling and complaining, Jake and Ellie put on their shoes and went outside.

"Where is he?" said Ellie.

"He's probably in his shed," said Jake.

> **POP QUIZ**
>
> What did Grandma want the children to do?
>
> ⓐ look for Grandpa
> ⓑ watch television

KEY WORDS

- **see** (see-saw-seen)
- **if**
- **find** (find-found-found)
- **all morning**
- **lunch**
- **be ready**
- **half an hour**
- **complain**
- **put on** (put-put-put)
- **probably**
- **shed**
- **do** (do-did-done)
- **cartwheel**
- **grass**
- **feel** (feel-felt-felt)
- **cool**
- **silky**
- **beneath**

"It's not so bad out here," said Ellie.

She did a cartwheel on the lawn.

The grass felt cool and silky beneath her hands.

Grandpa's shed was among some trees at the end of the lawn.

He spent hours in there.

He liked to invent things.

"I wonder what he's working on today," said Ellie.

Jake tried the door.

It was unlocked.

"That's strange," he said.

"Grandpa always locks the shed. `Aha!` Nobody else is allowed to go in."

KEY WORDS

- among
- at the end of
- spend (spend-spent-spent)
- there
- invent
- thing

- wonder
- work on
- try a door (*cf*. try)
- unlocked
- strange
- always

- lock
- nobody else
- be allowed to + *Verb* (*cf*. allow)
- go in (go-went-gone)

Ellie and Jake went into the shed.

It smelled of wood shavings and oil.

Grandpa was not there.

But something else was.

It looked like a sort of bicycle.

But instead of the front wheel, it had a metal box.

The box was covered with switches, knobs,
tubes, and wires.

The box was covered in thick, gray dust.

There was a separate, rectangular plate with three
dials and some numbers next to them.

Someone had written a message in the dust with
a finger.

The message was just three words:

HELP! RIDE ME

KEY WORDS

- into
- smell of
- wood shavings
- something else
- look like
- a sort of
- bicycle
- instead of
- front wheel
- metal
- be covered with
- switch
- knob
- tube
- wire
- be covered in
- thick
- gray
- dust
- separate
- rectangular
- plate
- dial
- next to
- someone
- write (write-wrote-written)
- just
- help
- ride (ride-rode-ridden)

1922 01 17
1969 05 12
1986 10 09
HELP RIDE ME

Comprehension Quiz

A Mark T for true or F for false.

❶ The house was new. T F

❷ The house was tall. T F

❸ The lawn was green. T F

❹ The shed was locked. T F

❺ Jake and Ellie were looking for Grandma. T F

B Fill in each blank with the right word below.

jobs	windows	flowers	birds

❶ The sun poured in through the ___________ of the house.

❷ ___________ were singing.

❸ The scent of ___________ filled the air.

❹ Mom and Dad could not give up their ___________ for the summer vacation.

 Choose the best answer to each question.

❶ Why was Ellie angry with Jake?

a) He said something rude to her.

b) He would not let her have the tablet.

c) He hit her.

d) He took her cell phone away.

❷ What was Grandma preparing?

a) breakfast   b) lunch

c) dinner   d) supper

❸ What did the shed smell of?

a) wood shavings and oil

b) dust and smoke

c) leaves and soil

d) metal and glue

❹ What had the message been written with?

a) a pen   b) a pencil

c) a finger   d) a computer

Chapter Two

Something Is Wrong

"What does that mean?" asked Ellie.

"Can't you read?" asked Jake, scornfully.

"Of course I can. But who wrote it?"

"I'm not sure. The writing is very wobbly.
I think that someone wrote it in a hurry."

"The only person who is allowed in this shed is
Grandpa," said Ellie.

KEY WORDS

- wrong
- mean (mean-meant-meant)
- ask
- read (read-read-read)
- scornfully
- of course
- sure
- writing
- wobbly

- think (think-thought-thought)
- in a hurry
- only
- person
- must + *Verb*
- find out
- climb onto
- bike (= bicycle)
- pedal

"It must be him," said Jake.

"But why would he need help?" asked Ellie.

"I don't know, but I'm going to find out." Aha!

Jake climbed onto the bike.

He began to pedal.

Jake pedaled the bicycle faster.

Some lights began to flash on the box.

"What are you doing?" cried Ellie.

"I don't know," said Jake, but he pedaled faster and faster.

The lights flashed green, and then yellow, and then red.

"What's happening?" shouted Ellie.

KEY WORDS

- faster
- light
- flash
- cry
- What's happening?
- shout
- disappear
- ghost
- see right through

- behind
- wait for
- leap
- toward
- grab hold of (*cf.* hold (hold-held-held))
- waist
- saddle
- enough
- sit on (sit-sat-sat)

Jake and the bicycle began to disappear.

Jake looked like a ghost.

Ellie could see right through him.

She could see the wall of the shed behind him.

"Wait for me!"

She leaped toward the bicycle and grabbed hold of Jake's waist.

The saddle was just big enough for the two of them to sit on.

STOP
1922 01 17
1969 05 12
1986 10 09
HELP
RIDE
ME

Then, everything began to look very strange indeed.

The wooden walls of the shed began to spin.

Then, they changed color from brown to green.

The air turned very cold.

A strong wind began to blow.

Something wet struck Ellie in the face.

It was snow.

"Stop pedaling, Jake!" she shouted.

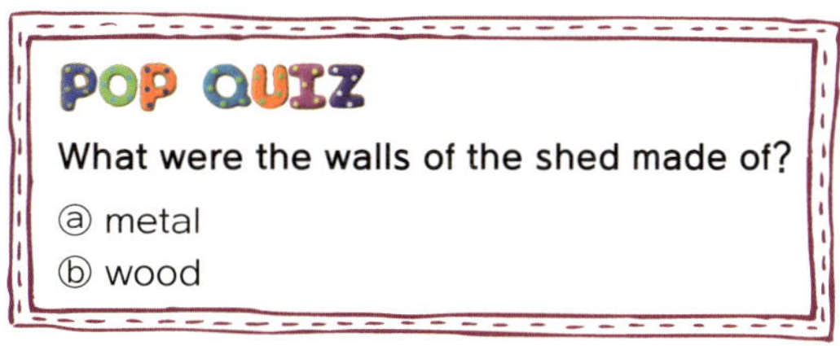

KEY WORDS

- everything
- indeed
- wooden
- spin (spin-spun-spun)
- from *A* to *B*

- turn
- strong
- blow (blow-blew-blown)
- wet
- strike (strike-struck-struck/stricken)

He stopped pedaling.

The walls stopped spinning.

Everything began to look more solid.

"Where are we, Jake?" whispered Ellie.

They were sitting among some trees.

It was dark.

Snow was falling.

Where was the shed?

Where was the beautiful summer garden?

"I don't know," said Jake.

"I want to go back," said Ellie.

"So do I," said Jake, "but I don't know how."

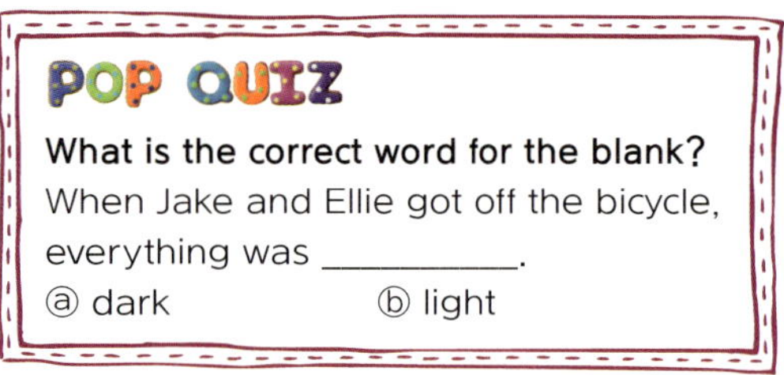

KEY WORDS

- more
- solid
- whisper
- dark
- fall (fall-fell-fallen)
- garden

- want
- go back (*cf.* back)
- So do I.
- shiver
- climb off
- wear (wear-wore-worn)

- thin (↔ thick)
- clothes
- push one's way
- edge
- deep

Shivering, the children climbed off the bicycle.

They were wearing thin summer clothes.

"We need to find out where we are," said Jake.

He and Ellie pushed their way through the trees.

They came to the edge of a lawn, covered with

deep snow.

"That's strange," said Jake.

"This looks like Grandma and Grandpa's garden."

"Yes," agreed Ellie.

"I can see the steps that lead up to the house."

"Everything's all right then," said Jake, smiling with relief.

"I don't know what's happened, but perhaps Grandma and Grandpa can explain."

KEY WORDS

- agree
- step
- lead up to (lead-led-led)
- all right (*cf.* right)
- smile with relief
- perhaps
- explain
- run ahead (run-ran-run)
- drink (drink-drank-drunk)
- warm
- shower
- race up to

Ellie ran ahead.

She wanted a hot drink and a warm shower.

She raced up to the door and went into the kitchen.

Jake ran in behind her.

"Something is wrong," whispered Ellie.

"This is not the right kitchen."

"Yes, it is," said Jake.

"There is the table, and there is the sink."

"But it is not the *same* sink," said Ellie.

"And where is the microwave?

Where is the oven and the dishwasher?"

She pointed towards one wall, where the oven usually was.

In its place was a black cooking range.

She had seen a picture of one in a history book.

"I will turn on the light," said Jake.

He went to the wall, where the light switch usually was.

In its place was a gas light.

Footsteps came along the corridor outside the kitchen.

"Someone's coming!" hissed Jake.

"Hide!"

KEY WORDS

sink (*cf.* sink
(sink-sank-sunk))
same
microwave
oven
dishwasher
point
towards
usually
place
cooking range
history
turn on
gas light
footstep
along
corridor
hiss
hide (hide-hid-hidden)

A Who said what? Match each line with the right character.

❶ 

- a) "What does that mean?"

- b) "Can't you read?"

❷

- c) "Why would he need help?"

- d) "I'm going to find out."

B Put the sentences in order.

❶ Ellie jumped on the bicycle behind Jake.

❷ Jake pedaled the bicycle faster.

❸ Jake and the bicycle began to disappear.

❹ The lights began to flash.

________ → ________ → ________ → ________

C Choose the best answer to each question.

❶ Why did Jake think that someone wrote the message in a hurry?

a) The words were not finished.

b) The words were not spelled correctly.

c) The writing was wobbly.

d) The words were difficult to read.

❷ What struck Ellie in the face?

a) rain   b) snow

c) leaves   d) wind

❸ Why didn't Jake and Ellie return home at once?

a) They wanted to explore first.

b) They had broken the bicycle.

c) They didn't know how to get home.

d) They were too tired to pedal anymore.

❹ Where were the footsteps coming from?

a) the corridor   b) the garden

c) the staircase   d) the shed

Chapter Three

A Time Machine

Ellie and Jake crouched behind the table.

A maid came in the kitchen.

She wore a black dress with a white apron over it.

She wore a white cap on her head.

"Who is she?" whispered Jake.

"What is she doing in Grandma's house?"

"I'm going to ask her," said Ellie, bravely.

She stood up.

"Who are you?" she said.

The maid jumped in fright.

"Who are you?" she cried.

KEY WORDS

- machine
- crouch
- maid

- apron
- cap
- bravely

- **stand up** (stand-stood-stood)
- **jump**
- **in fright** (*cf.* fright)

POP QUIZ
Who came into the kitchen?
ⓐ Grandma
ⓑ a maid

Jake decided to stand up, too.

"Tell us where my grandparents are," he said.

The maid seemed to forget her fear.

"You are only a pair of kids," she laughed.

"You gave me such a fright!

Where have you come from?

Why are you wearing such strange clothes?

I've never seen a girl wearing trousers."

Jake and Ellie looked at each other.

They did not know what to say.

"I'm going to call Mom and Dad," said Jake.

He keyed the number into his cell phone.

"There is no signal," he said.

"The battery needs charging, too.

It will not last much longer."

KEY WORDS

▪ decide	▪ laugh	▪ key
▪ seem	▪ such	▪ signal
▪ forget	▪ come from	▪ battery
(forget-forgot-forgotten)	▪ never	▪ last
▪ fear	▪ trousers	▪ much
▪ a pair of	▪ each other	▪ longer
▪ kid	▪ call	

Jake took the cable from his pocket.

"Where can I plug this in?" he asked the maid.

She looked confused.

"What do you mean?"

"Where are the plug sockets for the electricity?"
Jake asked again.

KEY WORDS

- cable
- pocket
- plug in
- confused
- plug socket
- electricity
- again

The maid laughed.

"Electricity? We don't have that here.

Only the rich people in London have electricity.

I am sure that the king has it."

"The king? What king?" asked Jake.

The maid laughed again.

"You are so funny," she said.

"King George V, of course!"

Jake's face went pale.

He leaned toward Ellie.

"King George V was on

the English throne

near the beginning

of the twentieth

century," he

whispered.

"I think that the bicycle is

a time machine.

We are still in the same house, but we have gone

back almost a hundred years."

"So Grandpa and Grandma are not even alive!"

said Ellie.

"Then who will help us?"

KEY WORDS

- rich
- people
- London
- king
- funny
- go pale

- lean
- be on the throne
- near
- beginning
- twentieth
- century

- still
- almost
- hundred
- even
- alive

The maid looked kindly at her.

"We have a telephone," she said.

"Follow me."

Jake and Ellie followed her to the door.

Looking into the hallway, they saw a table with a strange looking object on it.

It looked like a tall, black flower
made from hard, shiny material.
On the base was a circular dial
with holes in it.

▲ a candlestick telephone

Numbers were printed in the
holes.

Hanging from the side was another black thing
shaped like a cone.

"What is it?" whispered Ellie.

"It is the telephone, of course," said the maid. 

"I don't suppose you have ever seen one before.

Not many people have."

KEY WORDS

- kindly
- telephone
- follow
- hallway
- object
- made from
- hard

- shiny
- material
- base
- circular
- hole
- be printed
- hang (hang-hung-hung)

- side
- another
- shaped
- cone
- suppose
- ever
- before

Jake pulled the maid back into the kitchen.

"I need to ask you a question," he said.

"Have you seen an old man around here?"

"He's my Grandpa," added Ellie.

"He's in trouble and we must find him!"

"I'm sorry," said the maid.

"I haven't seen any old men here.

I think that it is time for you to leave now.

I will be in trouble if anyone finds me talking instead of working.

My mistress has just had a baby — a baby girl.

I must prepare some food for my mistress."

KEY WORDS

- **pull** (↔ push)
- **question**
- **around**
- **add**
- **be in trouble**
- **sorry**
- **any**
- **it is time for** + *Person* + to + *Verb*
- **leave** (leave-left-left)
- **anyone**
- **mistress**

- **have a baby**
- **prepare**
- **move**
- **take a photograph**
- **show**
- **gasp**
- **stare at**
- **be from**
- **circus**
- **magician**

Before she could move, Jake took a photograph of
her with his cell phone.
He held it up to show her.
"That's me!" she gasped.
"How did you...?"
She stared at Jake and Ellie.
"Are you from the circus or something?
You must be magicians!"

A Who said what? Match each line with the right character.

❶ 

a) "Tell us where my grandparents are."

❷ 

b) "Where have you come from?"

❸

c) "I'm going to ask her."

B Fill in each blank with the right word below.

cone	shiny	flower	circular

❶ The telephone looked like a tall, black ____________.

❷ The telephone was made from hard, ____________ material.

❸ On the base of the telephone was a ____________ dial with holes in it.

❹ Hanging from the side was another black thing shaped like a ____________.

C Choose the best answer to each question.

❶ Where were Jake and Ellie when the maid came into the kitchen?

a) by the oven

b) behind the table

c) in the cupboard

d) under the sink

❷ Why couldn't Jake call Mom and Dad on his cell phone?

a) He did not have his cell phone.

b) There was no telephone in the house.

c) He did not know their number.

d) There was no signal.

D Mark T for true or F for false.

❶ Only the king had electricity.   T   F

❷ There were no plug sockets in the house.   T   F

❸ Jake kept his cell phone cable in his pocket.   T   F

❹ The shed was a time machine.   T   F

Chapter Four

Familiar Faces

Jake and Ellie went outside again.
They ran down the lawn toward the trees.
The bicycle was waiting for them. Aha!
Jake bent over the dials on the front of the bicycle.

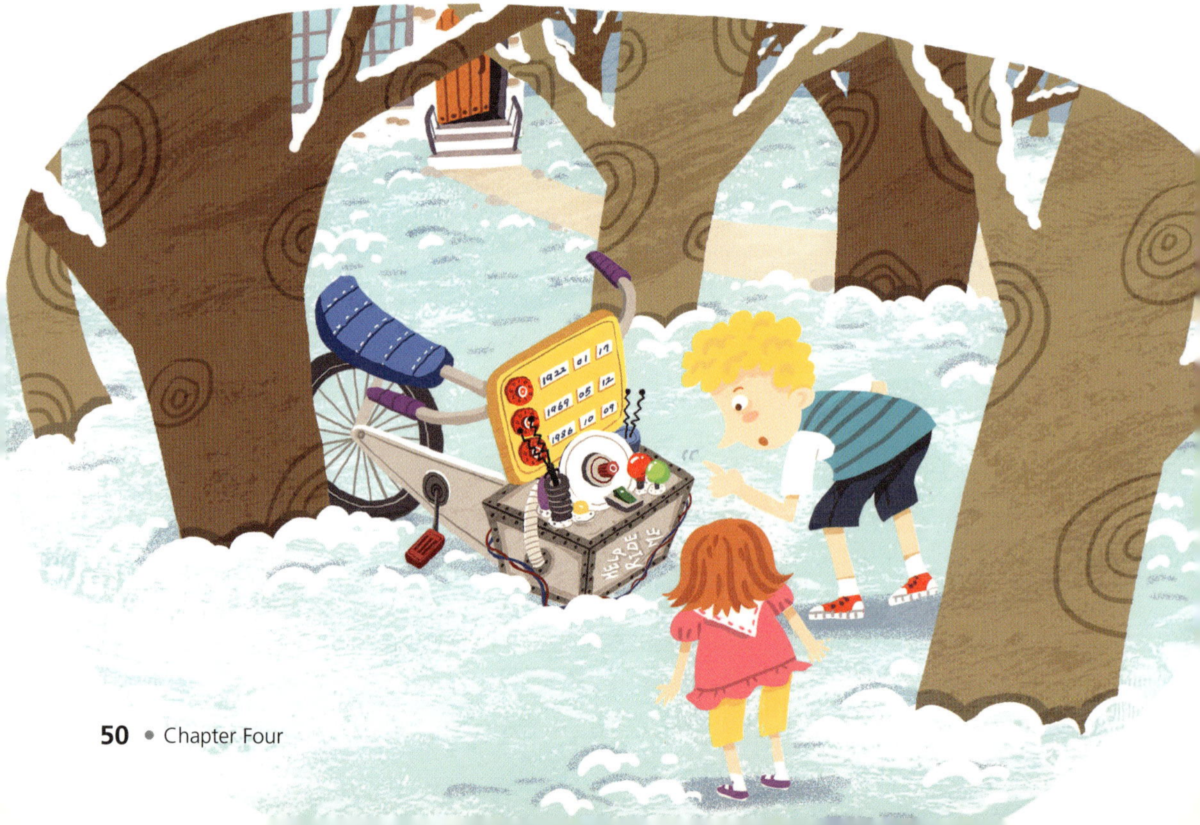

"Look," he said.

"We can turn them to choose a date.

There are three dials.

They are set to three different dates.

Grandpa must have chosen the three dates that
are showing.

The first is January 17, 1922.

The second is May 12, 1969.

The third is October 9, 1986."

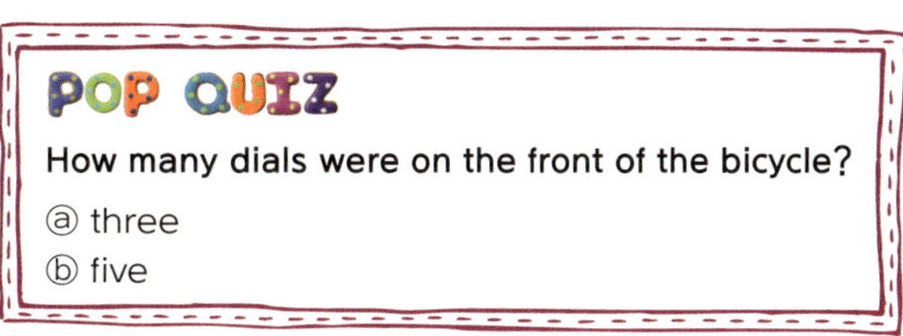

KEY WORDS

- familiar
- down
- on the front of
- **choose** (choose-chose-chosen)
- date

- **set** (set-set-set)
- different
- first
- January
- second

- May
- third
- October

"So the first is where we are now," said Ellie.

"I guess so," agreed Jake.

"But is Grandpa in 1969 or 1986?" asked Ellie.

"I don't know," said Jake.

"There is only one way to find out."

Ellie nodded, and climbed onto the saddle of the bicycle.

"This time, *you* can hang on behind," she said.

She began to pedal.

The trees began to fade and whirl.

Everything flashed light and dark, light and dark.

The air grew warmer and then colder again.

KEY WORDS

- guess
- nod
- hang on
- fade
- whirl
- grow (grow-grew-grown)
- warmer
- colder

1922 01 17
1969 05 12
1986 10 09
HELP
RIDE
ME

At last, everything stopped moving.

The same trees stood around them although they were taller.

The air was warm.

"Welcome to 1969," whispered Jake.

He and Ellie got off the bicycle and went toward the lawn.

A boy and a girl were playing there.

They were throwing a ball to each other.

A woman stood near the house.

She was pregnant.

She looked familiar.

"Come in now, children," she called.

"You can watch your television program while I take a rest."

Jake grinned.

"They have TV now," he whispered.

KEY WORDS

- at last
- although
- taller
- welcome to
- get off (get-got-gotten)

- throw (throw-threw-thrown)
- pregnant
- watch
- television
- program

- while
- take a rest
- grin

Jake and Ellie waited until the children had gone indoors.

Then, they crept up to a window and looked in.

The room looked similar to the one they knew.

But everything in it was different.

A telephone sat on a small table near the window.

It had a heavy receiver and a circular dial with numbers on it.

Instead of a large, flat-screen TV, there was a big, brown box.

It had buttons on the front and a small, gray screen in the center.

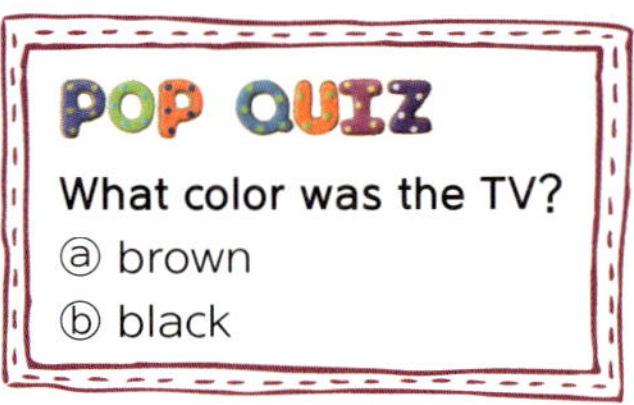

KEY WORDS

- until
- indoors
- creep up to
  (creep-crept-crept)
- heavy
- receiver
- flat-screen (*cf.* screen)
- button
- in the center
- sit down
- sofa
- press
- switch on
- remote control

As they watched, the girl and boy came into the room.

The girl sat down on the sofa.

The boy walked to the TV.

He pressed a button to switch it on.

"No remote control!" whispered Jake to Ellie.

When the TV came on, the screen was full of
black and white lines.

It made a crackling noise.

The boy twisted some wires on top of the TV.

"I've seen pictures of that," said Ellie.

"It is the aerial. Aha!

That is where the TV signal is
picked up."

Jake lifted his phone to
the window and took a
photograph.

▲ television antennas

KEY WORDS

- come on
- be full of
- line
- crackling
- noise
- twist

- on top of
- aerial (= antenna)
- lift
- about
- clear
- appear (↔ disappear)

- turn up
- sound
- open
- hear (hear-heard-heard)

The boy moved the wires about until a clear
picture appeared.

It was black and white.

"No color!" said Ellie.

The boy turned up the sound.

The window was open, so Jake and Ellie could
hear everything.

A news program showed a room.

Some pepople were staring at a huge machine.

It was covered with dials and switches.

"This computer can perform hundreds of

calculations," the newscaster said. 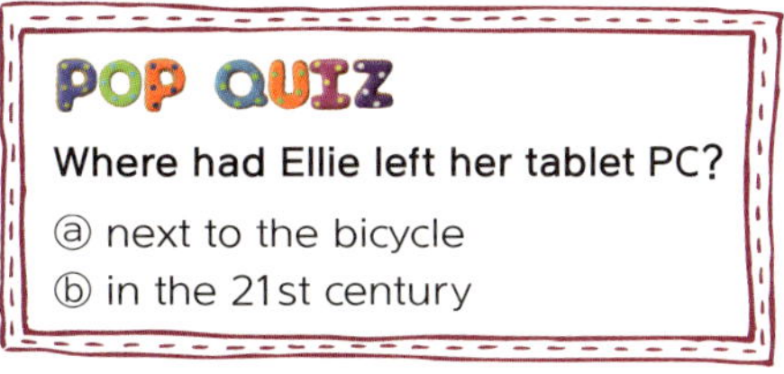

"Is that a computer?"

Ellie could not believe it.

"It fills the whole room!"

She thought about her tablet, which she had left

in the 21st century.

It was so small, yet it could do so much.

KEY WORDS

- news
- huge
- perform
- hundreds of
- calculation
- newscaster
- believe
- whole

"Do you think Grandpa is here?" said Ellie.

"I don't think so," said Jake.

"The bicycle was dusty when we found it.

Grandpa wrote the message in the dust.

It is not dusty where the bicycle is now.

Come on, let's try 1986."

Ellie wanted to talk to the children in the room.

They looked familiar.

She felt as though she knew them.

But it was more important that they find Grandpa

— and quickly. **Aha!**

She and Jake ran back to the trees.

But the bicycle was gone.

KEY WORDS

- dusty
- Come on!
- let's + *Verb*
- as though
- important
- quickly
- be gone

Chapter Four — Comprehension Quiz

A Put the sentences in order.

❶ Everything flashed light and dark.

❷ Ellie jumped onto the saddle of the bicycle.

❸ The air grew warmer and then colder.

❹ Ellie began to pedal.

________ → ________ → ________ → ________

B Complete the sentence by connecting each thing and its location correctly.

❶ The telephone was •　　　　　• a) on top of the TV.

❷ The aerial was •　　　　　• b) on the small table.

❸ The buttons were •　　　　　• c) near the window.

❹ The table was •　　　　　• d) on the front of the TV.

C Choose the best answer to each question.

❶ Which date did Jake and Ellie travel back to first?

a) June 6, 2016

b) October 9, 1986

c) May 12, 1969

d) January 17, 1922

❷ How could Jake and Ellie hear the TV program so well? Choose *two* answers.

a) They were hiding in the same room as the TV.

b) The boy turned the sound up.

c) The window was open.

d) They watched the program on Jake's cell phone.

❸ What was the "huge machine" that the people on TV were staring at?

a) a time machine

b) a computer

c) a robot

d) a weapon

Chapter Five

The Journey Home

"Where is it?" screamed Ellie.

They heard a metallic sound nearby.

It sounded like someone rattling a box of tools.

They followed the sound to a path in the garden.

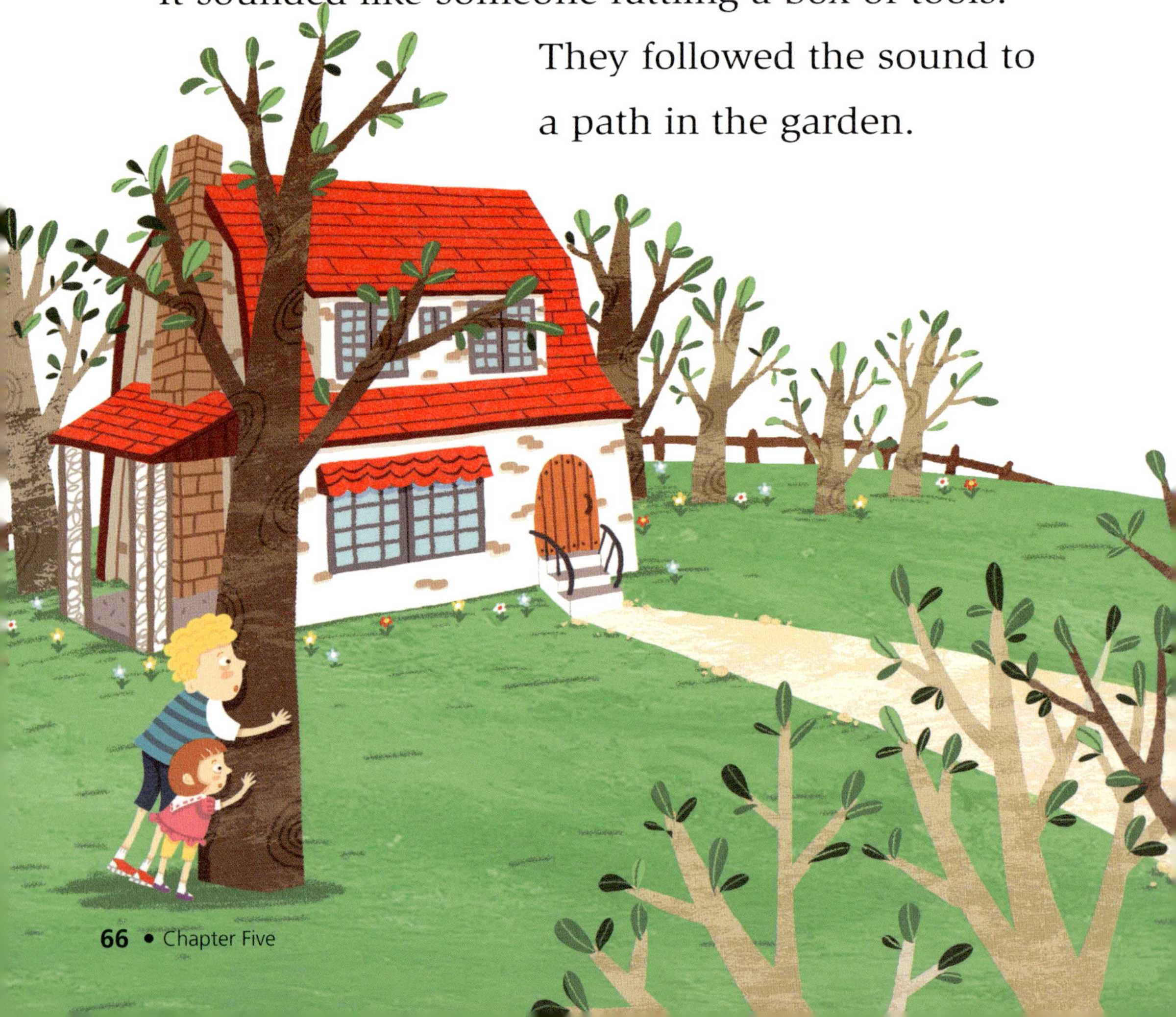

A man was there, bending over their bicycle.

"He must have found it!" gasped Jake.

"He's trying to figure out how it works!"

The man took a screwdriver from the box.

"What if he breaks it?" whispered Ellie.

"We will never get home!"

KEY WORDS

- journey
- scream
- metallic
- nearby
- rattle
- tool
- path
- figure out
- screwdriver
- what if ~?
- **break** (break-broke-broken)
- get home

Moments later, the boy came running across the lawn.

"Father!" he yelled.

"Mother says that the baby is coming!"

The man left the bicycle at once and ran after the boy, toward the house.

Jake leaped onto the saddle of the bicycle this time.

Ellie clung on behind.

Jake pedaled and the bicycle whizzed through time.

It only seemed like moments later that it landed with a thump.

They were still in the path, but the air was colder.

Leaves fell from the trees.

KEY WORDS

- moments later (*cf.* later)
- yell
- at once
- run after
- cling on (cling-clung-clung)
- whiz
- land
- with a thump (*cf.* thump)
- leaves
- fall from

1922 01 17
1969 05 ?
1986 10 12
10 09
HELP
RIDE
ME

They heard a man's voice.

"I need that document today," he said.

"Can you fax it to me?"

A young man appeared among the trees.

He was holding a black box to his ear.

It had an antenna coming out of the top.

Jake realized that it was a cell phone.

It looked really heavy.

"I know him!" gasped Ellie.

"It's that boy from 1969.

It is also Mom's brother, Uncle James!"

"So the baby born that year must have been Mom!" laughed Jake.

▲ a fax

(a device that changes images such as texts, pictures etc. into electric signals and transmits them through a telephone network to another device which prints out a copy of the original image)

KEY WORDS

- voice
- document
- fax
- antenna
- come out of
- realize
- uncle
- born (*cf.* be born)

Uncle James saw them and stopped speaking.

He frowned.

"Who are you?

Get away from our garden," he snapped.

"We're here to see… your father, Peter Simpson,"

said Jake.

That was Grandpa's real name.

In 1986, he was 44 years old.

Perhaps he could help.

"Why do you want to see him?" asked James.

"We…er…our grandfather sent us!" said Ellie.

It was true, after all.

Uncle James sighed.

"Follow me," he said.

He led them up the lawn to the house.

KEY WORDS

- **speak** (speak-spoke-spoken)
- **frown**
- **get away from**

- **snap**
- **be here**
- **real**

- **true**
- **after all**

They went into Grandpa's study.

On the desk was a computer, but it was a very old-fashioned one.

The monitor was big and heavy.

It sat on top of a box that had slots in it.

Next to the slots were some square things.

"Leave those floppy disks alone," warned Uncle James.

"My father has important data stored on them."

◀ a floppy disk

(Now people use USB, but people used to save data etc. to a floppy disk which they inserted into the drive on the computer tower.)

KEY WORDS

- study
- desk
- old-fashioned
- monitor
- slot
- square
- leave alone
- floppy disk
- warn
- data
- store

Another machine sitting on the desk began to hum.

It looked like a printer.

"Ah, that's the fax I've been waiting for," said

Uncle James.

A piece of paper went through the machine.

When it came out again, it had writing on it.

Ellie nudged Jake.

"We *must* find Grandpa," she said.

"I mean the 21st century Grandpa.

He needs our help."

Jake nodded.

"I think I know where to look."

He turned to Uncle James.

"We need to go," he said.

He lifted his phone and took a photograph of a startled Uncle James.

Ellie followed Jake outside.

"We need to see if the shed is here," said Jake.

"That is where he might be if he fell off the bicycle."

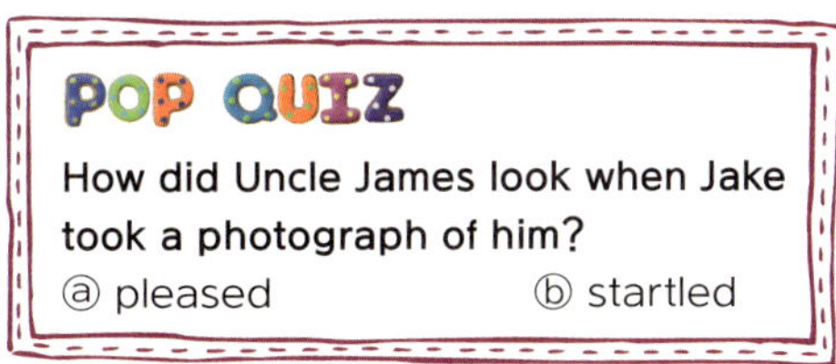

KEY WORDS

- hum
- printer
- a piece of paper
- go through
- nudge
- turn to
- startled
- fall off

He was right.

The shed stood in the trees, new and smelling of fresh paint.

Jake pushed the door open.

Inside, it was very dusty and smelled of smoke.

Grandpa — the one they knew from 2016 — lay on the floor, his eyes closed.

"Grandpa!" cried Ellie.

"We have come to help you."

Grandpa's eyes flickered open.

"Thank you," he gasped.

"I was pedaling the bicycle to 2016 and I fell off.

I hurt my knee and I could not get back on.

I needed help, so I wrote the message. Aha!

Then, I moved the pedals around with my hand.

The bike faded away without me.

It went to 2016, where you found it."

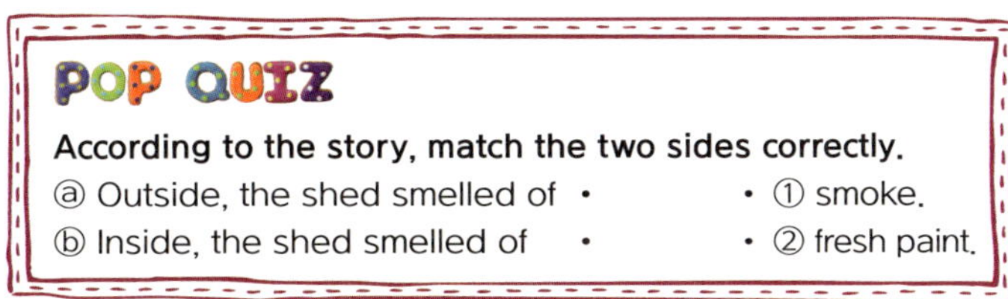

KEY WORDS

- fresh paint
- inside
- smoke
- lie (lie-lay-lain)
- floor

- closed (↔ open)
- have come to + *Verb*
- flicker
- hurt (hurt-hurt-hurt)
- knee

- get back
- fade away
- without

Ellie and Jake helped Grandpa to the area where the bicycle was waiting.

Grandpa and Jake squeezed onto the saddle.

Ellie sat on Grandpa's knee.

Jake pedaled, and the trees began to spin.

Leaves whirled around their heads.

Before long, they were back where they had started.

Ellie, Jake, and Grandpa sat together in the shed. They talked about everything that they had seen. They looked at the three photographs that Jake had taken on his cell phone.

"I know why you went back to 1969," said Jake.

"That's the year that Mom was born. But why 1986? And why 1922?"

"1922 was the year that *my* mother was born," explained Grandpa.

"So that was the baby girl that the maid told us about," said Ellie.

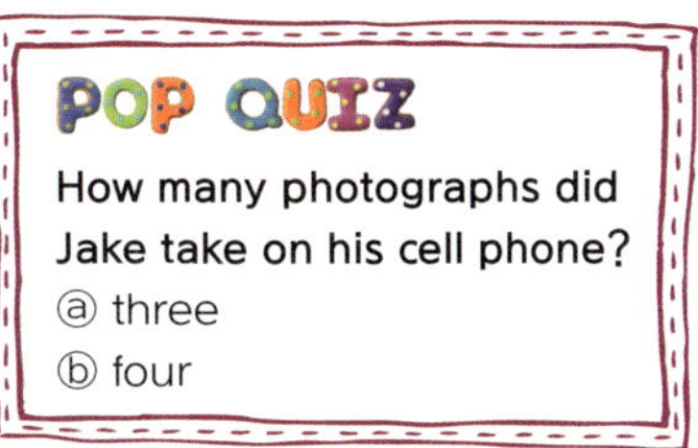

"1986 was the year that I first invented the time traveling machine," said Grandpa.

"It has taken me thirty years to build it.

I wanted to go back and tell my younger self that it worked."

"Did you meet him?" asked Jake.

Grandpa shook his head.

"I changed my mind.

It would be too strange for us to meet each other."

"What year will you travel to next?" said Ellie.

"I think I have had enough time travel," said Grandpa.

"But I haven't," said Jake.

"I want to see dinosaurs."

"I want to see knights and castles," said Ellie.

KEY WORDS

- thirty
- build (build-built-built)
- younger
- self
- meet (meet-met-met)
- shake one's head (shake-shook-shaken)
- change one's mind
- dinosaur
- knight
- castle
- in that case
- have to + *Verb*
- bigger
- go off
- adventure

"In that case," said Grandpa, "I will have to make the saddle bigger."

"Why?" asked Ellie.

Grandpa laughed.

"Because you're not going off on an adventure without me!"

Comprehension Quiz

A Fill in each blank with the right word below.

slots	paper	desk	disks

❶ On the ___________ in Grandpa's study was a computer.

❷ The monitor sat on top of a box that had ___________ in it.

❸ Important data were stored on the floppy ___________.

❹ A piece of ___________ went through the fax machine.

B Mark T for true or F for false.

❶ Grandpa lay on the floor with his eyes closed.　T　F

❷ Grandpa's eyes opened when Ellie spoke.　T　F

❸ Grandpa moved the pedals around with his foot after he was hurt.　T　F

❹ Grandpa sent the bicycle back to 2016 without him.　T　F

 Choose the best answer to each question.

❶ Why was the man bending over the bicycle?

a) He was trying to get on it.

b) He was trying to figure out how it worked.

c) He was trying to mend a broken part.

d) He was trying to take it apart.

❷ Who was the baby born in 1969?

a) Grandpa   b) Uncle James

c) Jake and Ellie's mom   d) Ellie

❸ Where did Jake and Ellie find Grandpa?

a) in his study   b) on the lawn

c) in the shed   d) in the kitchen

❹ Why did Grandpa want to make the saddle bigger?

a) so that it would be more comfortable

b) so that a dinosaur could sit on it

c) so that the bicycle could travel farther

d) so that he, Ellie, and Jake could travel through time together

Let's Review the Story

Fill in the blanks to review the story.

Title: The _______________ Bicycle

Main characters: J________ , E________ , and G________

Summary:

G________ is lost in time. Ellie, 7, and Jake, 9, must find him. They ride the t________ bicycle to find him.

- 1922

They travel to 1922 first. They explore Grandma and Grandpa's h________ in 1922. There is a t________, but there are no cell phones. And there is no e________ in the house.

- 1968

They travel to 1968 second. It is the year their mother was b________. The house has a TV now. But it's ________ and white. It also uses an ae________. And a c________ is as large as one room.

- 1986

They find Grandpa in 1986, the year in which he i________ the time machine. They also see a ________ phone, a f________ machine, and a desktop c________.

Let's Think & Talk

Think about the following questions and answer them freely.

❶ What periods in the past did Jake and Ellie visit on the time machine bicycle? What devices that they saw in each period are different from ones in the present? Organize them in order and say.

❷ If you could ride the time machine bicycle and travel through time, what period would you go to? Why?

❸ If you built your own time machine, what shape or functions would you add? Organize your thoughts and discuss your ideas with your friends.

Answers Let's Review the Story

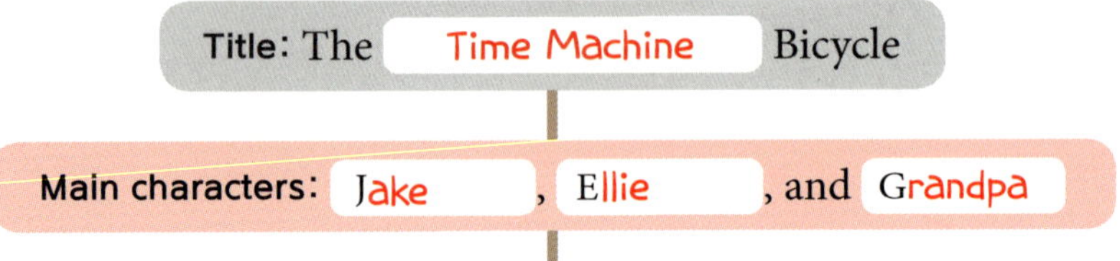

Summary:

Grandpa is lost in time. Ellie, 7, and Jake, 9, must find him. They ride the time machine bicycle to find him.

• 1922

They travel to 1922 first. They explore Grandma and Grandpa's house in 1922. There is a telephone, but there are no cell phones. And there is no electricity in the house.

• 1968

They travel to 1968 second. It is the year their mother was born. The house has a TV now. But it's black and white. It also uses an aerial. And a computer is as large as one room.

• 1986

They find Grandpa in 1986, the year in which he invented the time machine. They also see a cell phone, a fax machine, and a desktop computer.

After-reading Test

- **The Time Machine Bicycle**
- **Level 2**
- **17 Questions**

  (Vocabulary 4 / Reading Comprehension 10 /

  Sentence Structure & Grammar 3)

1. Which pair has the wrong past tense form of the listed verb?
    ① cut − cut
    ② read − read
    ③ hide − hide
    ④ hurt − hurt

2. Which pair has the wrong comparative form of the listed adjective?
    ① old → older
    ② cold → colder
    ③ big → biger
    ④ fast → faster

3. What is the correct word for the blank?

    > The box was covered ______________ switches and wires.

    ① with   ② away
    ③ toward   ④ through

4. What is the common word for the blanks?

    > • She leaped toward the bicycle and grabbed hold ________ Jake's waist.
    > • When the TV came on, the screen was full ________ black and white lines.

    ① up   ② on
    ③ with   ④ of

5. According to the story, what did Grandma NOT have when she was a child?
   ① a house   ② parents
   ③ a computer   ④ toys

6. What did Grandpa like to do in his shed?
   ① eat
   ② sleep
   ③ repair things
   ④ invent things

7. What happened when Jake pedaled faster?
   ① wheels broke
   ② lights flashed on the box
   ③ bells rang
   ④ ghosts appeared

8. What was located where a kitchen oven is usually put in the first place that Jake and Ellie arrived at?
   ① a sink
   ② a cooking range
   ③ a fireplace
   ④ a light switch

9. What had the maid never seen a girl wearing in the first place that
    Jake and Ellie arrived at?

① a skirt   ② a coat
③ trousers   ④ shoes

10. How far back in time did Jake and Ellie travel the first time they rode the bicycle?

① ten years
② twenty years
③ fifty years
④ almost one hundred years

11. What did the pregnant woman at the second place that Jake and Ellie went to
    plan to do while the kids were watching TV?

① prepare a meal
② take a rest
③ go for a walk
④ read a book

12. What program was airing on TV at the second place that Jake and Ellie went to?

① a comedy program
② a drama program
③ a news program
④ a children's program

13. What was Uncle James holding to his ear at the third place that Jake and Ellie went to?

    ① a cell phone   ② a fax machine

    ③ a radio   ④ a walkie-talkie

14. What part of Grandpa's body was hurt when he fell off the bicycle?

    ① knee   ② neck

    ③ hand   ④ foot

※ Choose the wrong part of the sentence. (15~16)

15.
> Wet something struck Ellie in the face.
>   ①   ②   ③   ④

16.
> I don't know, but I'm going to finding out.
>   ①   ②   ③   ④

17. What is the right sentence?

    ① Grandpa lock always the shed.

    ② Grandpa locks always the shed.

    ③ Grandpa always lock the shed.

    ④ Grandpa always locks the shed.

Memo

Memo 

Sarah J. Dodd
Sarah J. Dodd is an experienced primary school teacher who resides in the UK, but has also lived and taught in Australia. She has a PhD in Science and a certificate in Creative Writing. She has published several books for children: "An Angel Anyway" (Anyway Press, 2008) the "Little Angels" series (Lion Children's Books, 2009/10), "The Lion Picture Bible" (Lion Children's Books, 2015) and "Legs: the tale of a meerkat lost and found" (Lion Children's Books, 2015). Her poetry for children has also been highly commended and published in the anthology "Let in the Stars" (Manchester Metropolitan University, 2014).
She is currently working on further picture books for the very young, and a novel for older children.

The Time Machine Bicycle

Written by Sarah J. Dodd
Illustrated by Minjin Lee

First Published in February 2017

Editorial Manager: Juyon Choi
Editors: Kyunghee Jang, Jiyeong Park
Designer: Eunhee Lee
Cover Designer: Eunhee Lee

Published and distributed by

Darakwon Bldg., 64-1 Jandari-ro, Mapo-gu, Seoul, Korea 04031
Tel: 82-2-736-2031(ext. 250)   Fax: 82-2-732-2037
Homepage: www.ihappyhouse.co.kr
Publisher: Kyudo Chung

ISBN: 978-89-6653-507-1 18740 / 978-89-6653-156-1 18740(set)

[Components]
• 1 Audio CD (Recording Studio: Aram)
• Answer Keys & Korean Translation: Free download at www.ihappyhouse.co.kr